A PERSPECTIVES FLIP BOOK

The Split History of the

ATTACK ON PEARL HARBOR:

U.S. PERSPECTIVE

BY STEVEN OTFINOSKI

CONTENT CONSULTANT:
Tim Solie
Adjunct Professor of History
Minnesota State University, Mankato

COMPASS POINT BOOKS
a capstone imprint

Compass Point Books are published by Capstone,
1710 Roe Crest Drive, North Mankato, Minnesota 56003
www.mycapstone.com

LIBRARY OF CONGRESS CATALOGING-IN-PUBLICATION DATA

Names: Otfinoski, Steven, author.
Title: The Split History of the Attack on Pearl Harbor: A Perspectives flip book / by Steven Otfinoski.
Description: North Mankato, Minnesota: Compass Point Books, Capstone, 2018. Series: Perspectives flip books: Famous Battles | "CPB Grades 4–8." | Includes index.
Identifiers: LCCN 2017043018 (print) | LCCN 2017043856 (ebook)
ISBN 9780756556914 (library binding)
ISBN 9780756556952 (paperback)
ISBN 9780756556990 (eBook PDF)
Subjects: LCSH: Pearl Harbor (Hawaii), Attack on, 1941—Juvenile literature.
World War, 1939–1945—Causes—Juvenile literature. | United States—Foreign relations—Japan—Juvenile literature. | Japan—Foreign relations—United States—Juvenile literature.
Classification: LCC D767.92 (ebook) | LCC D767.92 .O79 2018 (print)
DDC 940.54/26693—dc23
LC record available at https://lccn.loc.gov/2017043018

EDITOR
JENNIFER HUSTON

MEDIA RESEARCHER
TRACY CUMMINS

DESIGNER
ASHLEE SUKER

PRODUCTION SPECIALIST
KATHY MCCOLLEY

IMAGE CREDITS

U.S. Perspective:

Alamy: Paul Fearn, 21, Sueddeutsche Zeitung Photo, 7; Getty Images: Bettmann, 16, Historical, 20, Keystone-France, Cover Bottom, MPI, 28, The Asahi Shimbun, 8; NARA: U.S. Navy, Cover Top, WAR & CONFLICT BOOK, 12, 15; Naval History & Heritage Command: 5, 11, 13, 24, 25; Shutterstock: Everett Historical, 19, 29; Wikimedia: NARA/U.S. Navy, 17

Japanese Perspective:

Alamy: PJF Military Collection, 29; AP Photo: 13; Getty Images: Keystone-France, Back Cover Top, Roger Viollet, 17, Underwood Archives, 24; Library of Congress Prints and Photographs Division: 27; NARA: U.S. Navy, Back Cover Bottom; Naval History & Heritage Command: 5, 11, 16, 21, 26, 28; Newscom: Pictures From History, 8, 12; Shutterstock: steve estvanik, 10 (all); Wikimedia: NARA/U.S. Navy, 19

Table of Contents

SHARED RESOURCES

CHAPTER 1

A MORNING TO REMEMBER

December 7, 1941 began as just another lazy Sunday at the Pearl Harbor Naval Base on the Hawaiian island of Oahu. Some early risers were already eating breakfast while other servicemen were dressing for church services. Many more were still asleep in their bunks on board ship or lying awake thinking about the leisure-filled day ahead of them.

About 30 miles (48 kilometers) away, at the Opana Point Radar Station near the island's northern tip, George Elliott and Joseph Lockard were on the job, scanning the skies on their mobile radar unit

U.S. Navy battleships were among the vessels docked at Pearl Harbor.

Suddenly, at 7:02 a.m., the two young Army privates noticed something odd on the radar screen. A big blip appeared to be heading southward toward Oahu at a fast pace. They assumed it was a large group of aircraft about 130 miles (209 km) away. As they tracked the blip, they called the information center at Fort Shafter to report the sighting. Lieutenant Kermit Tyler answered the call. He knew that a fleet of American B-17 bombers had left California the previous day and were due to arrive that morning. Tyler assumed this was what was showing up on the radar screen. But the information about the bombers was classified, so he decided not to share it with the two privates. He simply said to them, "Don't worry about it."

Satisfied that there was no cause for concern, Lockard and Elliott went to breakfast when their replacements arrived. When they last tracked the blip, it was just 22 miles (35 km) from Oahu.

Soon after, Rear Admiral William R. Furlong aboard the ship *Oglala* looked up and saw what American servicemen called the "red meatball" on the side of an approaching plane. It was the Rising Sun symbol of Imperial Japan. This was no drill or the arrival of friendly aircraft from California. This was a very real attack by 183 Japanese planes. Moments later, naval operations officer Logan Ramsey was shouting into a loudspeaker for all to hear, "Air Raid Pearl Harbor!"

A HISTORY OF HATRED

The sneak attack on Pearl Harbor was the climax of anti-American feelings that had been brewing among the Japanese for nearly a century. It began in 1853 when U.S. battleships under the command of Commodore Matthew Perry anchored near Tokyo and forced Japan to sign a diplomatic agreement with the United States. This "opening" of the proud, isolated kingdom led to Japan being forced to trade with Western nations. Humiliated by these events, Japan resolved to transform itself into a world power that could compete economically and militarily with the United States and Europe. Japan achieved this goal and set out to show off its military strength in wars with China (1894–1895) and Russia (1904–1905), both of which Japan won.

In late 1937 Japanese troops invaded Nanking, China, and brutally massacred approximately 300,000 soldiers and civilians.

Following World War I (1914–1918), members of an international conference in Washington, D.C., were concerned about Japanese aggression in Asia, so they set limits on the nation's manufacture of weapons and warships. Again humiliated, the Japanese resolved not to let the Western powers intimidate or bully them. In 1931 Japanese troops invaded the Chinese province of Manchuria and by 1937 were attacking other parts of China.

A NEW WORLD WAR

Nazi Germany had sparked World War II (1939–1945) in September 1939 when it invaded Poland. The United States had stayed out of the war but supported the cause of the Allies, which included Great Britain and France, who were fighting Germany and Italy.

Japanese soldiers entered French Indochina in September 1940 and invaded more of the country the following year.

In 1940 Japan joined Germany and Italy against the Allies, forming the Axis Powers. Japanese forces soon marched into French Indochina, present-day Vietnam. Japan's ultimate goal was to take over all of Southeast Asia, and the U.S. commonwealth of the Philippines. Alarmed by this move, the United States froze all Japanese assets in the country in 1941. This meant that the Japanese government couldn't access any funds or resources it owned that were invested in American banks or businesses. The United States also launched an embargo on Japan. As a result of these moves, Japan lost access to high-quality scrap metal and fuel for airplanes, which were needed to continue the fight with China. U.S. President Franklin D. Roosevelt was hopeful that these tough measures would bring the Japanese to the negotiation table, but they were no longer interested in negotiating. Japan's leaders were preparing for war against what they saw as their sworn enemy—the United States.

WARNING SIGNS

The Pearl Harbor attack should not have come as a complete surprise to the United States. There had been warning signs going back nearly a year. In January 1941 Joseph Grew, the U.S. ambassador to Japan, heard a rumor about a planned attack on Hawaii. Grew told his superiors, but they considered the rumor unreliable and ignored it. In September the U.S. Navy intercepted a coded message from Tokyo, the Japanese capital, to the Japanese consulate in Honolulu, the Hawaiian capital on Oahu. The message asked the consulate to note the location of U.S. ships docked at Pearl Harbor. It took U.S. authorities a month to decode the message, but it was never sent back to those in charge at Pearl Harbor.

On the very morning of the attack, another Japanese message was intercepted that was meant for Japanese ambassador Kichisaburo Nomura telling him to announce a break in relations with the United States and destroy his code machine. When Army Chief of Staff George C. Marshall received the message, he immediately tried to alert the commanders in Hawaii. But because of technical problems, his warning didn't arrive until hours after the attack had taken place.

CHAPTER 2

THE FIRST ATTACK

Seaman First Class Leslie Vernon Short was at his machine-gun station aboard the battleship USS *Maryland*. He was writing Christmas cards to the folks back home when he saw a swarm of Japanese planes soaring overhead. "I broke out ammunition nearby, loaded my machine gun and opened fire . . .," Short later said. "Flames and smoke burst from the first plane I aimed at. . . . I think I also hit the second plane which I aimed at . . . but by then I was so busy that

A reconaissance photo taken by the Japanese showed U.S. warships lined up on Battleship Row.

The U.S. Navy had eight battleships stationed at Pearl Harbor. Seven of them, including the *Maryland,* were anchored on the eastern side of Ford Island in the heart of Pearl Harbor. Known as Battleship Row, this was the first target for the attacking Japanese planes. Lined up two by two, the battleships were sitting ducks for the enemy bombers.

The USS *Arizona* was docked two ships away from the *Maryland* on Battleship Row. High up in the crow's nest of the battleship, Seaman First Class Vernon Olsen had a perfect view of the attacking planes and their pilots. "We just stood there and watched them fly right between the masts and bomb us," he later recalled. "You could see their faces. You could see them grinning when they were firing at us."

Within minutes, a 1,760-pound (798-kilogram) bomb had struck the *Arizona* in its forward section. Two chief officers standing on the bridge were among those killed instantly. The bomb ignited the magazine below deck that contained more than a million pounds (453,590 kg) of gunpowder. It exploded in a huge fireball. The ship jumped 15 to 20 feet (5 to 6 meters) into the air and then quickly sank to the bottom of the harbor. During the explosion, hundreds of sailors were blown off the deck and into the water. Many others leaped from the ship's burning decks into the harbor. Among them was sailor Carl Carson who recalled: "I didn't know how bad I was hurt. And I got

When a bomb hit the magazine of the USS Arizona, *the ship exploded, killing hundreds of men instantly.*

out there about 10 feet [3 m] and I guess I must have passed out . . . and I saw this bright light and something made me come to. And so I got back up to the surface of the water and . . . the oil was a fire all around . . . the fire was approaching me, wasn't but two feet from me and he [another sailor] reached down and pulled me up out of the water. And that man saved my life."

Carson was one of the lucky ones. Of the 1,500 officers and crew aboard the *Arizona,* only 335 survived. Many who weren't killed instantly by the explosion were trapped below deck in their bunks and drowned. Others burned to death when they leaped into the fiery waters that were coated with oil spewing from the ship's punctured fuel tanks.

None of the other six exposed battleships escaped the relentless bombing. The *Oklahoma* was struck by nine torpedoes and leaned so badly that it capsized, drowning 429 men. The *West Virginia,* which was anchored just north of the *Oklahoma,* was hit by six torpedoes and also leaned badly. It managed to stay upright, but it still sank 40 feet (12 m) to the harbor's bottom.

Of the 105 crew members who died on the *West Virginia,* the grimmest casualties were those who survived more than two weeks before they died. They were trapped below deck and suffocated because rescuers were unable to reach them. The *California,* like the *Arizona,*

The USS Maryland *(left) and the capsized USS* Oklahoma

sank when its magazine exploded from a bomb hit. The *Maryland* and *Tennessee* also suffered damages and casualties.

At the end of Battleship Row, a single torpedo tore a hole in the *Nevada*'s bow, the front of the ship. But it was still able to function, so its surviving first officer, Lieutenant Commander Francis James Thomas, made the bold decision to start moving the ship out of the harbor. However, the stricken ship didn't have enough power to go anywhere. The eighth battleship, the *Pennsylvania,* was across the harbor in dry dock and out of harm's way . . . for the moment.

A second target for the attackers were the six airfields on Oahu. It was crucial for the Japanese to destroy as many grounded planes as they could to prevent American pilots from taking off for a counterattack. Hardest hit was Hickam Field, just south of Pearl Harbor. The planes were lined up wing to wing to prevent sabotage on the ground. But this interlocking formation actually made the planes easy targets for the Japanese pilots.

Both men and planes on the airfield were fired upon. Like many members of the Army Air Corps at Hickam, Technical Sergeant Joseph A. Pesek ran for his life across the bullet-filled airfield. "I . . . almost made the edge of the runway when three more planes came at me," Pesek said. "They were so low that I could see the ground kicking up where their machine-gun bullets were hitting. I hit the ground again, covering my head with my hands. It seemed as though a thousand things passed through my mind, mostly of home and my family. I could not believe it when those three planes passed right over without hitting me."

Some 121 personnel were killed at Hickam and another 274 were wounded. Of the 57 airplanes on the ground, 18 were destroyed and many of the others were seriously damaged. Of the other five airfields, Wheeler was hit the worst, with 54 planes lost and 37 men killed.

By this time, despite the chaos, confusion, and blinding smoke and fire, some Americans were joining Seaman Short in fighting back. Numerous men at Hickam, including Pesek, lined up at the hangar to grab rifles and fire them at the enemy planes overhead. Four men set up an old World War I machine gun on a tripod and fired at the planes from the exposed runway. Not long after, the men received a direct hit from a Japanese plane and were blown to bits.

Hickam Field was extensively damaged by the Japanese attack.

Chief Petty Officer John William Finn

At Kaneohe Naval Air Station, Chief Petty Officer John William Finn also used a machine gun to fire at the enemy from the open runway. Although he never knew if he hit any planes, Finn kept firing for the entire attack. He received many wounds, including a deep scalp cut from flying metal. Finn was later awarded the Medal of Honor for his bravery during the Pearl Harbor attack.

At the height of the battle, a fleet of American B-17s called Flying Fortresses appeared in the skies over Pearl Harbor. One serviceman thought they were Japanese reinforcements. But in fact they were the bombers flying in from San Francisco that Lieutenant Tyler had mistaken the Japanese for several hours earlier. However, they carried no ammunition and could not fight back. Miraculously, only one of them was shot down by the Japanese.

At about 8:30 a.m., just over half an hour after they had arrived, the Japanese planes departed. They left a scene of total destruction behind them. The damage done to ships, planes, and personnel was devastating. But there was more to come.

The rear of a B-17 Flying Fortress was hit by Japanese gunfire as it landed at Hickam Field. Miraculously, the entire crew survived.

PEARL HARBOR

Native Hawaiians called the harbor "Wai Momi," meaning Water of Pearl, because until the late 1800s, the harbor was full of pearl-producing oysters. In 1887 Hawaiian King Kalakaua gave the United States exclusive rights to Pearl Harbor as part of a trade agreement. America annexed Hawaii in 1898, and by 1908 Congress had authorized a naval base there.

The base grew in size and importance over the years. In the spring of 1940, President Roosevelt decided to move the U.S. Pacific Fleet there from San Diego, California. He felt having a large presence in the Pacific would deter the Japanese from attacking other Asian countries. Little did he know that it was the Pacific Fleet itself that would soon be the target of Japanese aggression.

CHAPTER 3

THE SECOND WAVE

A strange silence settled over the skies above the fiery nightmare of Pearl Harbor. But it lasted less than half an hour. Shortly before 9 a.m. a second wave of Japanese planes appeared in the smoke-filled skies. Once again, they had specific targets to hit. One of these was the only battleship that had escaped damage in the first attack—the dry-docked *Pennsylvania*. The enemy dropped several bombs near the battleship, but only one made a direct hit. Twenty-eight men were killed and 29 were wounded.

The *Cassin* and the *Downes,* two destroyers alongside the *Pennsylvania,* were not as fortunate. A dive-bomber put a hole in the *Cassin*'s fuel tanks and burning oil spewed out onto both it and the *Downes.* The *Downes* was also struck by a torpedo. Ammunition on both ships was ignited and exploded, engulfing them in flames. A short distance away, a third destroyer, the *Shaw,* was hit three times by bombs and set ablaze. The *Shaw*'s crew evacuated the ship at 9:25 a.m. Five minutes later its magazine exploded.

Meanwhile, the *Nevada,* under the command of Lieutenant Commander Thomas, was ready to remove itself from the line of fire. Chief Boatswain E.J. Hill leaped off the ship and cast off the lines. As the battleship began to move away, Hill jumped into the water and swam back to the battleship, dodging gunfire every inch of the way.

The USS Shaw *exploded in a fireball after its magazine was struck by Japanese bombs.*

But the Japanese were not about to let the *Nevada* get away. Dive-bombers struck the ship multiple times before it reached the channel. One of the 57 men onboard who were killed by the bombs was E.J. Hill, who was attempting to anchor the ship when he died. After his death, he was awarded the Medal of Honor for his bravery. Meanwhile, Thomas realized that if his ship sank at the entrance of the channel, it would block the way for all but the smallest vessels trying to get out of the harbor and into the open sea. With the help of two tugboats, Thomas beached his ship at Waipio Point, just south of the channel. Because of his quick thinking, a number of ships were able to make it safely out of the harbor.

The USS Nevada *was heavily damaged but returned to action in late 1942.*

This was little consolation for Husband Kimmel, commander of the Pacific Fleet. Kimmel, who was at his home when the attack began, was only able to get as close to the combat as his office on base. Through a large window he watched helplessly as the Japanese destroyed his fleet. At one point, a bullet crashed through the window and grazed his jacket. Staring at the mark it left on his chest, Kimmel murmured to another officer, "It would have been merciful had it killed me."

By 10:00 a.m. the second wave of Japanese planes had departed as suddenly as they had arrived. The attack was over, leaving destruction and chaos in its wake.

AMERICA'S FIRST PRISONER OF WAR

Kazuo Sakamaki

Before the airplanes arrived, the Japanese had launched five two-man minisubs to attack U.S. warships with torpedoes. American ships sank two of the subs, and two others disappeared and were discovered on the sea bottom years later. One of these was partially destroyed by its own explosive charge, but the reason for the other's sinking was never fully determined. The fifth sub went off course and was abandoned by its crew. One crew member of this sub drowned and the other, Ensign Kazuo Sakamaki, was tossed onto the shore unconscious. He was soon captured and became America's first prisoner of war (POW) in World War II. When Admiral Isoroku Yamamoto heard of Sakamaki's capture, he threw a fit. Yamamoto was furious with Sakamaki for allowing himself to be taken prisoner, as this was thought to bring disgrace on the nation. Rather than be taken prisoner, Japanese soldiers were expected to commit suicide, a practice known as hari-kari.

Sakamaki spent the entire war in POW camps in several states. When he was released after the war, he returned to Japan, married, and became a successful executive for the Toyota Motor Company. He wrote a book called *I Attacked Pearl Harbor*, which described his experiences as a POW. His abandoned sub was found during the war and put on display in a traveling exhibit that raised money for the war effort. He saw it once on a visit to the United States. Sakamaki died in 1999 at age 81.

Chapter 4

In Disaster's Wake

The toll of the Japanese attack at Pearl Harbor was devastating, both in human lives as well as ships and planes. Some 2,335 military personnel were either killed instantly, died of injuries, or were missing. An additional 1,143 service members were wounded. Sixty-eight civilians died and 103 were wounded. Eighteen warships, including seven battleships, were sunk or seriously damaged. Of the 400 airplanes on the island, 188 were

The dead cannot be brought back to life, but ships, even if badly damaged, can be rebuilt. Three ships—*Arizona, Oklahoma,* and *Utah*—were sunk and were total losses. On the *Arizona* alone, 1,177 men were killed. Many were trapped inside and quickly burned to death. The ship was left resting at the bottom of the harbor, a permanent memorial to the men who died on board. The *Utah* also lies partially submerged at the bottom of the harbor. The *Oklahoma* was raised and scrapped. The other ships in Battleship Row and the destroyers, *Cassin* and *Downes,* were repaired and back in action by the end of the war. As for the lost planes, most of them were out-of-date and ready to be replaced by newer, better-designed aircraft.

RESCUE EFFORTS

Efforts to rescue the men aboard the sunken and capsized ships began immediately. Naval yard workers toiled around the clock to cut through the hull of the *Oklahoma* to rescue the men trapped inside. It was a race against time since the air supply would soon run out and the men would suffocate or drown in incoming water. Seaman Stephen B. Young, one of the men still alive on the *Oklahoma,* vividly recalled his ordeal 50 years later: "I could almost feel the dark. The stillness of that deep and stinking place pressed down over us all. I felt I was smothering in the darkness . . . [E]very so often, I became aware of the barely perceptible sound of the water as it rose, ever so slowly. . . ."

Crews worked to rescue the men trapped inside the USS Oklahoma.

Soon the men heard another sound—the pounding of a powered hammer on the outside of the ship. The men's joy at knowing that help was near was tempered by the grim reality that as the hull gave way, water would flood in. They might drown before they could be saved. As Seaman Young remembered: "We were as high in the compartment as we could go. . . . The hammer stopped and retreated. Our fingers grasped at the metal to pull it back with our bare hands. . . . [T]he difference between life and death was to get that piece of steel bent back so we could get out. . . . Now the hole was open, just wide enough for us to scrape through! It was just in time. The water was up to our chests and shoulders, flooding faster and faster. . . ."

The rescue workers and many others showed remarkable courage on December 7 and the days that followed. Sixteen Medals of Honor were awarded to those individuals, with 10 of them given to people who had died in the attack.

Printed in the United States 3945

DORIS MILLER

Doris Miller

African-American serviceman Doris Miller did not receive a Medal of Honor for his courage under fire because of racism in the United States. In fact his actions might have been forgotten if not for the persistent efforts of African-American newspapers. Because of those efforts, in May 1942, Miller was awarded the Navy Cross, then the third highest medal given by the Navy. He was the first black serviceman to receive the award.

When the attack came, Miller was doing laundry on the *West Virginia*. He raced to the bridge, and while dodging enemy fire, he pulled the ship's mortally wounded captain and other crewmates to a safer place. Then he manned a 50-caliber antiaircraft gun that he had no training to shoot and began firing at the Japanese planes overhead. "It wasn't hard," he said. "I just pulled the trigger and she worked fine." Miller's aim was good enough to bring down at least two Japanese planes and possibly as many as six. He only abandoned the sinking ship when he ran out of ammunition.

After the attack, Miller was promoted to cook third class, one of the few positions that most black servicemen at the time could aspire to. On November 24, 1943, he was killed on board the aircraft carrier *Liscome Bay* when it was struck by a Japanese torpedo in the Gilbert Islands. He was just 24 years old. In 1973 a warship was named the USS *Miller* in his honor.

CHAPTER 5

A NATION AT WAR

The news of the attack on Pearl Harbor stunned the nation. Many Americans feared this was just the beginning of a major invasion. Hawaii braced itself for more Japanese planes. There were even fears that the enemy would next strike on the west coast of the U.S. mainland. Fortunately, those fears proved groundless.

In Washington, D.C., President Roosevelt met with his advisers and cabinet members throughout the afternoon. Everyone agreed that the United States should declare war on Japan immediately.

Roosevelt prepared a speech that would be broadcast live to the nation via radio the following day. In the speech, Roosevelt planned to ask Congress to declare war on Japan. All the president's speechwriters were out of town for the weekend, so he had to write what was likely the most important speech of his presidency without their help. As he read through the finished speech, the wording in the opening sentence bothered him. He referred to December 7 as "a date which will live in world history." He felt the words "world history" weren't strong enough for this terrible attack. So he changed it to "a date which will live in infamy." It was a phrase that lives on to this day.

But President Roosevelt would not be the first public figure to speak out about Pearl Harbor. His wife, Eleanor, was set to deliver her weekly radio address the evening of December 7. It was not the speech she had expected to give only 12 hours earlier.

"I am speaking to you tonight at a very serious moment in our history . . .," she began. "Whatever is asked of us, I am sure we can accomplish it. We are the free and unconquerable people of the United States of America."

The following day at 12:30 p.m. President Roosevelt mounted a podium and faced an audience that included members of Congress, the Supreme Court, cabinet members, and other invited guests. "Yesterday, December 7, 1941 . . . the United States of America was suddenly and deliberately attacked by naval and air forces of the Empire of Japan," he began. He spoke little about the attack itself and the loss of life, vessels, and planes. Many of these details were still being learned. Instead, Roosevelt emphasized the positive need for action. "No matter how long it may take us to overcome this [planned] invasion," he said, "the American people in their righteous might will win through to absolute victory. . . . "

On December 8, 1941, President Roosevelt asked Congress to declare war on Japan.

He ended by urging Congress to pass the declaration of war.

The president's speech lasted only six and a half minutes, but he said everything that he needed to say. Both houses of Congress met behind closed doors to vote on the resolution. By 3:25 p.m. the Senate and the House of Representatives had both signed the declaration of war. The Senate voted 82–0 for war against Japan; the House voted 388–1. The sole vote against the resolution came from Congresswoman Jeannette Rankin from Montana, the first woman elected to Congress and a committed pacifist, a person who believes that war is wrong.

The president signed the resolution at 4:10 p.m. America was now in the war it had watched from the sidelines for more than two years. Great Britain declared war on Japan the very same day to show its support of the United States; so did Canada, Australia, and New Zealand. Several Latin American nations followed suit the next day. Germany and Italy, Japan's partners in the Axis Powers, declared war on the United States on December 11.

The war against the Japanese in the Pacific would be a long and challenging one. But through it all, American servicemen and women would be spurred on by the battle cry: "Remember Pearl Harbor!"

THE USS *ARIZONA* MEMORIAL

After it sank during the attack on Pearl Harbor, the USS *Arizona* was not recovered from the water. Because of the hundreds of dead crew members who remained on the sunken vessel, it was felt fitting and proper to leave it as a sacred burial place for the dead. An official memorial was completed in the harbor above the *Arizona* in 1962. It is now part of the World War II Valor in the Pacific National Monument.

Other sites on Pearl Harbor include memorials to the USS *Oklahoma* and the USS *Utah* and parts of Battleship Row and Ford Island. The Pearl Harbor Visitor Center includes two museums with artifacts from the attack and other battles of World War II. Visitors can only reach the *Arizona* Memorial by a U.S. Navy-operated boat. One of the most compelling features of the Pearl Harbor Visitor Center is a sculpture called the Tree of Life, a symbol of peace.

The wreck of the USS Arizona *can be seen just below the surface at the memorial.*

INDEX

GLOSSARY

AMBASSADOR—a government official who represents his or her country in a foreign country

ANNEX—to incorporate into a country or state

BRIDGE—the control center high on the forward section of a ship

CASUALTIES—people killed, wounded, or missing in battle or war

COMMONWEALTH—a country that rules itself but maintains ties to a larger nation

DRY DOCK—a dock where the water can be drained to repair ships

EMBARGO—an act by a government stopping trade to or from another country

EMBASSY—place where the government representatives of another country work

INFAMY—a lasting, widespread, and deep-rooted evil reputation brought about by something criminal, shocking, or brutal

INTERCEPT—to stop the movement of an object

MAGAZINE—a room aboard a ship where ammunition and explosives are stored

NEGOTIATIONS—discussions in order to come to an agreement

RECONNAISSANCE—scouting an area

SUFFOCATE—to die from lack of air

INTERNET SITES

Use FactHound to find Internet sites related to this book.

Visit www.facthound.com

Just type in 9780756556914 and go.

TIMELINE

1853

U.S. battleships commanded by Commodore Matthew Perry force Japan to sign a trade agreement with the United States

1894–1895

Japan defeats China in the First Sino-Japanese War; this victory demonstrates Japan's transformation militarily as a world power

1904–1905

Japan defeats Russia in the Russo-Japanese War; in doing so, Japan becomes the first Asian country to defeat a European power in modern times

1921–1922

Several countries meet at the Washington Naval Conference and sign multiple treaties; these treaties set limits on the manufacture of weapons and warships in Japan and other countries

1931

Japan invades the Chinese province of Manchuria

1941

JULY 24: Japan invades French Indochina (present-day Vietnam) with the goal of taking over all of Southeast Asia and the Philippines

AUGUST 1: The United States issues an embargo on exports of oil and fuel to Japan

SEPTEMBER: The U.S. Navy intercepts a coded message from Tokyo asking the Japanese consulate in Hawaii to note the locations of U.S. warships at Pearl Harbor

DECEMBER 7:

6:10 A.M.: Japanese fighter planes take off from aircraft carriers and head toward Pearl Harbor

7:02 A.M.: Using radar, George Elliott and Joseph Lockard notice what appears to be a large group of aircraft headed toward Pearl Harbor; they call Fort Shafter and are told not to worry about it

7:33 A.M.: U.S. Army Chief of Staff George Marshall receives a message intended for the Japanese consulate telling him to break ties with the Americans and destroy his important documents; Marshall tries to warn authorities in Hawaii, but the message doesn't arrive in time

7:55 A.M.: The attack on Pearl Harbor begins

1937

The Second Sino-Japanese War begins

1937–1938

During December 1937 and January 1938 an estimated 300,000 Chinese soldiers and civilians are killed when the Japanese Imperial Army invades the city of Nanking, China; the event becomes known as the Nanking Massacre

1939

SEPTEMBER 1: Germany invades Poland

SEPTEMBER 3: World War II begins when Great Britain, France, Australia, and New Zealand declare war on Germany

1940

SEPTEMBER 27: Japan, Germany, and Italy sign an agreement forming the Axis Powers

8:10 A.M.: The USS *Arizona* is hit by a bomb and explodes in a fireball; the ship quickly sinks, taking 1,177 men to a watery grave

8:30 A.M.: The first wave of the attack ends

8:54 A.M.: Another wave of Japanese planes begins a second assault on Pearl Harbor

10:00 A.M.: Japanese planes head back to their aircraft carriers; the attack is over

DECEMBER 8: The United States and several other countries declare war on Japan

DECEMBER 11: Germany and Italy declare war on the United States

1945

AUGUST 6: A U.S. plane drops an atomic bomb on the Japanese city of Hiroshima, killing at least 78,000 people

AUGUST 9: The United States drops a second atomic bomb, this time on the city of Nagasaki, Japan, killing 40,000 people

SEPTEMBER 2: Japan surrenders and World War II is over

Select Bibliography

Arroyo, Ernest. *Pearl Harbor*. New York: MetroBooks, 2001.

Gillon, Steven M. *Pearl Harbor: FDR Leads the Nation into War*. New York: Basic Books, 2011.

Hillstrom, Laurie Collier. *Defining Moments: The Attack on Pearl Harbor*. Detroit, Mich.: Omnigraphics, 2009.

Nardo, Don, ed. *Pearl Harbor*. San Diego.: Greenhaven Press, 2003.

Shirley, Craig. *December 1941: 31 Days that Changed America and Saved the World*. Nashville, Tenn.: Thomas Nelson, 2011.

Stille, Mark. "Yamamoto and the Planning for Pearl Harbor." *The History Reader*. http://www.thehistoryreader.com/modern-history/yamamoto-planning-pearl-harbor/

Stokes, Henry Scott. "Forty Years Later, Japanese Pilot Recalls Pearl Harbor." *The New York Times*. http://www.nytimes.com/1981/12/07/world/40-years-later-japanese-pilot-recalls-pearl-harbora.html

Willmott, H.P. *Pearl Harbor*. London: Cassell Co., 2001.

Further Reading

Allen, Thomas B. *Remember Pearl Harbor: American and Japanese Survivors Tell Their Stories*. Washington, D.C.: National Geographic, 2015.

Edwards, Sue Bradford. *The Bombing of Pearl Harbor*. Minneapolis, Minn.: Abdo Publishing, 2016.

Fitzgerald, Stephanie. *Pearl Harbor*. North Mankato, Minn: Capstone Press, 2018.

Johnson, Robin. *Pearl Harbor*. New York: Crabtree Publishing Company, 2014.

Critical Thinking Questions

1. There were warnings about the coming attack on Pearl Harbor. What were they, and why do you think that they were ignored by the United States? Use evidence from the text to support your answer.

2. What reasons did some Japanese officers have for wanting to attack Pearl Harbor a third time? Why did their superiors not agree? Based on the evidence and expert opinions, do you think the Japanese made a wise decision?

3. If the Japanese had not attacked Pearl Harbor and had avoided conflict with the United States, do you think the U.S. would have stayed out of World War II? Why or why not? Give reasons for your answer based on the text and your own thinking.